CLUSTERING RHYMES
A BOUQUET OF ARTY POEMS

FIROZ TATA (WOLFY)

XpressPublishing
An imprint of Notion Press

No.8, 3rd Cross Street,CIT Colony,
Mylapore, Chennai, Tamil Nadu-600004

Copyright © Firoz Tata (wolfy)
All Rights Reserved.

ISBN 978-1-63606-871-8

This book has been published with all efforts taken to make the material error-free after the consent of the author. However, the author and the publisher do not assume and hereby disclaim any liability to any party for any loss, damage, or disruption caused by errors or omissions, whether such errors or omissions result from negligence, accident, or any other cause.

While every effort has been made to avoid any mistake or omission, this publication is being sold on the condition and understanding that neither the author nor the publishers or printers would be liable in any manner to any person by reason of any mistake or omission in this publication or for any action taken or omitted to be taken or advice rendered or accepted on the basis of this work. For any defect in printing or binding the publishers will be liable only to replace the defective copy by another copy of this work then available.

I would like to dedicate this book to those who claimed to love me, but were never dedicated and strong enough for the same. Without them I wouldn't learn about what true love-connection may be.

Thank you for bestowing a life-long cherished sorrow without which I wouldn't have ever attempted to start writing poetries.

Your ever to hardly loving,

Firoz

Contents

Preface   *vii*

Acknowledgements   *ix*

1. We Together	1
2. A Blessing In Disguise	2
3. Precious Pen	4
4. Dear Heart	5
5. My Home, Sweet Home	6
6. Faith, Patience & Nerve	8
7. Nightmare	9
8. Story Of Her Life	11
9. Ecstasy: The Great Happiness	13
10. Hoping Queen Forever	15
11. An Innocent Inner Child	17
12. Can't Stop Loving You	19
13. They May Call It Love	21
14. Mindless Thoughts	23
15. Why I Once Fell In Love?	24
16. Never Meet Ever	26
17. Real Imagination	27
18. Before It's Too Late	28
19. Scared, Scarred, Shining She	30
20. My Melting Shackles	32
21. His Lady	34
22. Notion Of An Ideal Nation	36

Contents

23. Fitness	37
24. Sweeper's Story	39
25. Beauty And The Wolfy	41

Preface

I feel blessed in bringing my inventive poems to the frontage by placing into your hands my first poetry book, 'Clustering Rhymes'. In times of uncertainty and unpredictability, I fell in love to pen down my deepest feelings in the form of verses, creating beautiful poems. I am confident that this collection of poems will help in creating a spectacular vision about my views in the minds and hearts of my readers.

Accurate vocabulary and rhyming words are the influential tools through which one can portray their innermost reflection of self, soul and emotions. I too have tried my best to express my mind through various poignant and painless verses.

'Clustering Rhymes' is a book that tranquilise some of the deepest thoughts that keeps spinning in my head. Before starting the journey of creating this book, little was I aware of the fact that it would not only help me to vent out my views into stanzas but also help me to get into the shoes of several others who might not have got an opportunity to express what they feel within their innermost selves. Hence, I believe, this book will not only help in sharpening and augmenting the ingenious horizons about love, hopes and beauty, but will also enlighten readers to express their feelings fluently.

Special efforts are made to select appropriate vocabulary making all poems coherent and lucid in their reading and understanding. I hope my book will not only touch your minds and hearts, but will also touch your souls and lives in general.

PREFACE

Let me assure you that this publication will go a very long way in increasing your fondness for poems and further assist you to cultivate a writing flair. I have no doubt that this book will be welcomed equally by all, especially, literature and poetry lovers. It will be a moving experience for the readers.

Last but not least, I feel great happiness to make my readers aware of the fact that the interior file and the cover page of the book is designed by me with the help of a beautiful Interior Formatting Tool and Cover Creator provided by Notion Press. It was a challenging, learning and a wonderful experience altogether.

With these words, I take great pride and privilege in opening the doors of my fascinating world of poetries.

- The Poet

Acknowledgements

From deep down my heart, I love to express my sincere gratitude to my beloved mother Ms. Heera Tata to raise my spirit during the journey of creating my first poetry book, and as always, providing me with complete isolation.

Not to forget acknowledging my beautiful poet-sister Ms. Harshada (Zenith), to suggest me with the amazing title and sub-title of this book.

I would also love to extend my heartfelt gratitude to Notion Press for providing an encouraging platform of Xpress Publishing, helping me to self-publish this wonderful poetry book.

Last but not least, I also want to thank every single individual who says, "You have to read Wolfy's poetries" to their family members, friends and relatives.

- **The Poet**

1
We Together

We have just walked some path of life together,
We still have a long way to go further, forever.
You discovered some good parts of me,
And I still have so much to show and see.

We have hiked together in same life direction lane,
We have not yet danced and drenched in thundering rain.
We have celebrated each other's pleasures and delights,
We have yet not partnered each other's pains and frights.

I want to live with you, sob with you and get old with you,
I just want our every wish and dream come true.
Holding your hands, I want to enjoy that sunrise view,
Even at last sunset, I want our love to stay fresh and new.

Ups and downs be there; together we will solve,
We may never be perfect; with every passing day we will evolve.
Hurricanes and hurdles, I promise; together we will stand,
Darling we'll love each other until our eternal end.

2
A Blessing in Disguise

—♡—

At 12/13, a bizarre day arrives in her life,
A strange gut pain, piercing innocent her like a knife.
Uneasiness sieges the body; compelling it to change,
Shattered, socked and scared; discovering her first red stain.

Filled with confusions and terror; heading down,
Mother comforting, a part of 'His' bestowed crown.
A divine blessing in every woman's path,
Isn't easy, hardly prepared to learn this new birth.
A sad experience; full of restrictions,
A monthly period, full of reprehensible rules and regulations.

With the birth of her puberty,
Forbidden stepping in religious places;
Stretching borders in her own home.
Outlawed and secluded in a room;
Confining freedom to roam.
Taboo to touch; restricting her to pray,
Unbelievably true;
Existence of such norms until today!

FIROZ TATA (WOLFY)

Ah! Until when? Until when? Until when?
Simple biological process with which only women blessed,
Taking menstruation as a matter of shame and stress.
Hiding in disgrace; wrapped-rolled in a piece of cloth-paper,
Discomfited, depressed and dejected for the red stained diaper.
Ashamed and shy for the special seven menses days,
Shedding silent tears for 'His' monthly miracle praise.
Unaccepted by ignorant inconsiderate men and society.
Ah! Until when? Until when? Until when?

Instead of comforting and making her feel secured,
Merely giving her a tag of 'dirty and impure'.
It's now or never; kicking out the folly faiths,
Accepting it as a normal event, and not silly myths.

My men, my brothers and dear husbands,
It's time for utmost care, love and warmth to your women.

ppp

3
Precious Pen

Oh! My precious pen, what a close mate you have been to me,
You felt my solitude and vexation that no one could see.
You experience my glee, you feel my agony,
I windbag with my words, but you never get stony.

I conceive words through you when I am happy and gay,
You are like my loyal spouse to share sadness and secrets.
If you had eyes, my fables would make you ha-ha and spin,
For now, I have no one so intimate just as a brief on my skin.

I use you when I am low; portraying my qualms and fears,
I know, you'll be by my side as sad as me when I drop my tears.
If you had a soul, you would have cried with me,
I have no one as strong as you to steer me out of this salty sea.

Have been there with me from the time I learned to hold you,
You viewed my desires and dreams; the delighted devil chewed.
If you had emotions, you would have embrace my frail part,
Precious pen, for now I have no one to mend my broken heart.

4
Dear Heart

Dear 'Heart', though time won't always remain the same,
Your outside beauty is not always going to stay.
Time will come, your thick black hair will turn thin and grey,
Tight and fair skin will wrinkle day-by-day.

Surely I'll keep kissing your fabulous forehead,
Madly love and indeed care the same way.
I may not be always so humble and kind,
Someday, I might be grumpy, harsh and a sweet swine.

My blood pressure may shoot and my temper may incline,
Finding ways to love, I'm dumb; still, will you always be mine?
Dear 'Heart', tell me that no matter whatever circumstances;
We will keep loving one another above spaces and distances.

I may not be flawless and my success won't always sustain,
My brain may find itself in trauma to never meet you again.
Love let-down may turn me insane; giving me acute heartache,
Still dear, will you hold my hand to help me breathe again?

♥♥♥

5
My Home, Sweet Home

My childhood cage, teen's prison,
Adulthood Carandiru Penitentiary poison.
Hugs and love like a needle in a haystack,
Empty pockets, delicious cuisine; dignity under daily attack.
Home systems unsystematic; rest always at unrest,
What more I could do...
To make everything little best?
My home, sweet home!

Lunches dinners unstable, unhappy and dark,
Dogs lucky than my human bark.
Brighter black days,
Deserted wretched nights,
What more I could do...
Before surrendering all my might?
My home, sweet home!

Cleanliness next to Godliness; a sweet dream to dream,
Years passing by, they only loved delicious cream.
Sleep stolen, my peace into pieces,
Shower in a terror and entertainment in my earpieces.

FIROZ TATA (WOLFY)

What more I could do...
Besides creating this poem to the creator?
My home, sweet home!

I love to hate and hate to love,
Day-by-day, I am a lion chocking in a magical glove.
Welcoming home is a fright filled with shame,
They love to play mindless game.
What more I could do...
Besides telling someone the feelings of my pain?
My home, sweet home!

ppp

6
Faith, Patience & Nerve

In a few weeks apart; needed you more than ever,
I felt your whiff in the musty air like a loyal lover.
I imagined your presence more than the previous occasion,
I value your existence more than anyone.

Chipper voice, blossoming fresh morning feelings for you,
'Good morning' still whisper from a woman, I can't glue.
Captivating, I firmly believed; only she's my peppy jig,
Searched since warm winds whistled through the tree-twigs.

Wedged in the brutal branches of an old oak tree,
She wanted me to set her flying and free.
The experience was marvellous and once in a life time,
Loving a right yet wrong woman almost similar to my chime.

Wherever we go, whatever we do; life will bring us together,
Destined Universe will bless me to be her child's stepfather.
The mighty power of two hearts to realise the depths of love,
We'll fill those unhealed hearts with faith, patience and nerve.

♥♥♥

7
Nightmare

It was so solitary and creepy,
My surroundings felt so weepy and sleepy.
My shadows left; invading blackness,
Forcing to bow my head in blindness.

I could hear the distant gongs of grandfather's clock,
A sound that felt so loud from the above clouds.
Voices shrieking; I am dead and unwanted,
Until body-blood burnt my heart, haunted.

I felt the vile whisper in the hushed winds,
Couldn't see anything destined towards my ruins.
The dripping sounds of drizzle went louder and brasher,
Until I closed my ears to cover.

I squawked and yelled.
"Please, stop for Heaven's sake".
The fiend smiled; saying no, shaking his hideous head.
I didn't knew why I was going through this,
Several sharp sibilant sounds were making hiss.

CLUSTERING RHYMES

Oh! This was the place one never wanted to be in,
Dejection, distress and darkness added to my night's misery.
I couldn't hold this nightmare any longer,
Lord please help me to get out of this torture.

༄༄༄

8
Story of Her Life

Once upon a time:
They seemed to love each other a lot,
Will never get apart, was their thought.
Marriage they used to celebrate,
Plights of life they wanted to eliminate.

Starting a family was their dream,
Conceiving made their hopes deem.
The reasons were unknown,
Hitting their hearts like a stone.

A strong feeling for a baby made him feel uneasy,
He started to become loud and grumpy.
Blame games turned into squabbles,
It gave invitation to future troubles.

Soon he found someone worthy,
Who could birth him a baby.
She caught him with another mate,
Started cursing her unfortunate fate.

CLUSTERING RHYMES

You deserve better, her inner voice whispered,
Opted a new life forgetting how much she suffered.
Moving on that's what she wanted to do,
Time is the best healer she proved.

One day, she met someone,
He was her dad's best friend's handsome son.
Months passed, they come closer,
Started sharing stories with each other.

They took oath of being together, forever,
Started tasting each other's lips' honeyed flavour.
Soon she got blessed with a cute angle,
Her life's long awaited dream became real.

One fine day, she encountered her ex,
He looked pale, dejected and vex.
His woman had fled with someone young,
He regretted his folly decision.

He confessed his blunder, asked to forgive,
Uttered his desire to be once again together-live.
But it was too late to repent now,
She had already become someone else's crown.

❦❦❦

9
Ecstasy: The Great Happiness

Ecstasy is all about gratification,
One may get from one's action.
Ecstasy from good or bad deeds,
It is related to an emotion that breeds.

Seeing the rainy clouds in the sky,
The peafowl gets joyous and high.
Spreading out its mesmerizing tail,
Eager to dance and displays its train.

When the page of summer turns,
Souls start to less burn.
Roaming raindrops rhythmically kisses the earth.
And a new nature starts to birth.
A poor peasant's hard work and thankless agony,
Hardly feeds his family and that's the sad irony.
Seeing at the fluttering crops in his field after years,
Jam-packs his eyes with joyous tears.

CLUSTERING RHYMES

Ecstasy is a feeling or state of great happiness,
Eliminating life's bleakness into brightness.
Ecstasy has countless potent forms,
Depends on us; to bring it out even through life storms.

❦❦❦

10
Hoping Queen Forever

Flashing flashbacks:
That May Sun drenched in the West,
Those stunning days, I felt truly blessed.
The warm winds whistled through my soon to be grey hair,
Quaking hopes kissed horizon; sowing my first love affair.

Through the prickly woods a path I tried so hard,
Beneath chest, my heart pounced out of its yard.
Against my wish grass blades started to bleed,
When a yield of love Moon decided to breed.

Ahead of me was a heavy weight to uphold,
Strong inner voices valour me, starting my first love-mould.
Almost there, too far yet too close,
Her golden guiltless gaze made me a lover-rose.

A woman warrior, no doubt about that,
A tattoo cuddling her right leg.
Beautiful brown eyes; soft silken palms,
Once I'll surely hold her in my strong wide arms.

Authentic smile, tranquil semblance; I let her within,
My rock-strewn love adventure began.
Into a fire lit orchard; rode like a furious fiend,
I'll win by rescuing the unsafe Queen.

They say, the path I am on is wrecking wrong for me,
I still smile and reply, "Why don't you wait and see?"
Only when the unfinished business is set and done;
The world will realise, hopes never died,
My Queen, destined forever to be fantasized.

༄༄༄

11
An Innocent Inner Child

Hello dear:
Years fly by, grown from a child to an adult,
The deceptive world appears as a result.
Parting apart the innocent inner child within,
Staying stainless, cheerful and grin.

I come across my inner child quite often,
He loves and pampers me when I am forgotten.
He keeps me generous, virtuous and hilarious.
My heart and soul feels pious, joyous and fabulous.

He sustains my ethics up and high,
Instils joy when I eat candies and chicken pie.
At times I curse him for the tenderness he portrays,
People feel pride spitting venom sprays.

When I get horrified and my heart thumps,
My inner child holds me before someone dumps.
He teaches me how to be bold,
I stride strong through his scold.

CLUSTERING RHYMES

He reads me like none, appears like an alien.
Loves me like special someone.
This poem is a small homage to him,
Urging you all, discover your innocent inner child within.

❦❦❦

12
Can't Stop Loving You

Dearest sister:
Someone who will comprehend me; may be!
Someone who knows the way I feel; may not be!
In every situation her concern is very real,
In every season, nursing my deadly febrile.

Times when she would see me down and out,
Her innocent heart would nearly bleed and shout.
If everybody had an elder sister so sweet and witty,
Would feel a divine heaven on Earth full of knotty.

To have a sister like her; so selfless and sacrificing,
A woman bestowed forever, so loving and embracing.
A blood bond that diminishes never; so smoother,
Who is generous, gentle and patient, like a second mother.

A rare tie; deep, vibrant and profound,
With so much affection, nowhere else to be found.
Though my love feelings are seldom expressed,
True siblings endure and survive every life-test.

CLUSTERING RHYMES

Care and compassion towards her, rests in my heart,
She is my soul's primary part.
Sometimes unloved, unheard, underrated;
She'll be always there when my life needs to be calibrated.

As we mature, our feelings grow deeper and fonder,
Sometimes she silently smacks me as hard as a bar bouncer.
One thing is as sure as a death...
A sister is an inseparable cologne and breath,
Who at times is also responsible to...
Hurt me! Hurt me! Hurt me!
My beautiful 'Chicken' sibling,
God chose for life-long caring and sharing.

♥♥♥

13
They May Call it Love

The blind love:
Something so magical in the air; tied by an invisible string,
Something so matchless like a solitaire unique ring.
Something so outlandish but so very alluring,
Setting her so apart; for my heart's sewing.

I shufti around the party,
Glancing through the gathering.
I kept on discovering seductress splendour,
But not as witty-winsome; God's beautiful sender.

My eyes found that rubicund angelic face once more,
Hands shivered and heart pounced out of its core.
My breath stood fixed and a few heartbeats missed,
Pondering. What was so elegantly unusual? I hissed.

Graced, simple and amiable woman in a white gown,
Looking less than her age, sparkling like a silver swan.
Was it the divine look, or her walk urbane?
Was her free soul ready to fly out of the chained cage?

CLUSTERING RHYMES

Though she was feeling miserable; I believed,
Her ill-fated story, I hardly disbelieved.
Now she caught my gaze on her flawless face,
Fair cheeks blushed ruddy and she felt little embarrassed.

I glanced again and again finally pacing off,
And rode towards my house.
Mortified of making her conscious,
A feeling in me aroused, a man more ambitious.

I couldn't stop thinking, her hypnotizing brown eyed persona,
And pretty palms in black gloves, forgetting Ramona.
Her face failed to escape my mind,
I couldn't recognize my emotion; they may call it love!

ppp

14
Mindless Thoughts

Drizzling rain; drenching waver mind,
Blazes of quivering thoughts making me blind,
Trying hard to search pleasant esplanade,
Why do we have to always depend on fate?
Submerging the mind with curious thoughts,
Envisaging bright future without thinking a lot.
Failures lashing like a thunderstorm,
Feat after creepy clouds, bringing hope-ray, making me warm.

Despair hits like a heavy hail with lightning,
The home of acidic criticism is so frightening.
Burning in a fire of rage,
Retribution upsurges in my mind's backstage.
Finding self in a snare with obnoxious smell,
Can you hear my final warning bell?
Let's be cautious at every step,
Behind spurious smiles is a hidden hideous trap.
My aching heart shrieks to surrender,
I squeal to fight when I don't see the world of splendour.

15
Why I Once Fell in Love?

I woke up today, first thought came about her.
Can't see tears mixed in her love for liquor.
Deity's best creation, my stabbed heart whispered,
It's hard to hold my love-hatred backward.

Silhouette of beauty had changed,
Her allure became black, blue and damaged.
Wondering why my heart is still acting bizarre,
Her thoughts still makes me shiver.

Her malicious smile gave me chills in spine,
Ill-advised mind still believed, she'll be only mine.
Appearing to be invisible yet visible bond,
Echoing like an electrifying time bomb.

Every moment she dwelt in my mind,
My veins gushed aloud,
How can someone be so ruthless and unkind?

Scintillating eyes like shining stars,
Buried aches in her several scars.

FIROZ TATA (WOLFY)

A treasure with a wicked pleasure,
Once upon a time, my joy of myriad measures.

Touched to bruise my heart forever,
Are my feelings so folly to keep loving her?
Wondering what is this dumbness called,
Why I once fell in love? My heart recalls.

▷▷▷

16
Never Meet Ever

I felt for you...
The first time I got charmed by your unique sight,
I felt connected with you...
The first time we chatted until that late moonlit night.
I felt special, the time you seeded me first forehead kiss,
I felt cared the first time you wiped my tears, I couldn't miss.

I felt safe, the first time you walked holding my hand tight,
I felt proud to have you...
The first time you took my stand to fight.
I felt loved, the first time you vowed me to be forever by my side,
I felt Universe as mine...
The first time I hugged you from the back on that bike ride.

Blustery feelings felt in that short span of first wine and dine,
Many more yet left to feel with spaces of time.
We were surely destined to love and live together, forever.
Then abruptly, lost eternally to never meet ever.

♡♡♡

17
Real Imagination

A hypnotic speech is telling me,
I'll float on a silver star reflecting deep sea.
Instead my mind is flying far and high,
Beneath the scorching sun in wide blue sky.
It said I'll sail in a wrecking small boat,
Ha-ha! I laughed, I am too high for no gloat.
To be ashore by these simple words,
Now I am soaring with a flock of beautiful birds.
It's hardly possible devil is going to find me,
For what he says is not what I see.
I deceive him towards my decisive way,
I want to sightsee and seize the beautiful day.
Bare free feet and now barely a youth,
I know where I am and that's the only truth.
Life gives a serious punch and low blow,
My family and friends always so close.

♡♡♡

18
Before it's too Late

If someone we aren't talking,
Had only a few hours before chocking,
What would we say?
No point of waiting,
When those few hours have started end-racing.

Storming emotions in which we drawn,
When somebody we madly love lets us down.
Moments and memories repetitive in mind,
We fail to accept why they were so unkind.
Was this worth in the end?

Words are left unspoken,
Hours turn into weeks.
Before we realize,
Months turn into peaks.
We hold on to something, for years.
But how would we feel, if the end was near.

Imagine how a best buddy felt,
Not speaking to that friend over something petty,

Being told their friend passed away, sleeping on a settee.
Imagine how a son felt,
Upset with his parents, not saying ,"I love you back",
Only to find out they perished on a railway track.

If reading this brought someone special into your mind,
Tell that person how you feel until life is little kind.
While there is still time,
Make your life a sweet chime.
Life is too short, regret can be too long.
How will you feel when that person is gone?

May be reading this poem was a fate.
Tell that person how you really feel,
Before it's too late! Before it's too late!

19

Scared, Scarred, Shining She

It was so deadly dangerous of her attraction,
Deciding to seduce him through her arid addiction.
Deep enigmatic eyes; a lotus woman amidst bricks,
Sizzling bold bod, making him a love-lunatic.

Owning several bizarre secrets and divine fragrance,
Sting by societal honeybees and husband's alliance.
Holding several accounts of misery and pain,
Scared, scarred, shining she who never wanted to gain.

Never prayed a poisonous prince with his silver bonanzas,
Needed a warrior wolfy with several love song stanzas.
Sensing the sunshine and moonlight; fighting for his beauty,
Holding her safely as his priceless possession and responsibility.
Powering the impossible into possible,
The passionate possibility of the power of connection incredible.

She was the first shining satellite of his wrecking world,
And probably the last.

FIROZ TATA (WOLFY)

In a million years; and million more to come,
Was and will be only one Moon until the Earth blasts.
She bestowed a life-long love gift to him,
A pleasure that ends with either end, eternally.

▷▷▷

20
My Melting Shackles

I had a beautiful dawn in my life,
Was out in the sky, still without a wife.
I had wide wonderful wings, I can say,
They were too sturdy and in a colourful glace.

I glided high up in the sky with sulking eyes,
I dared to rip apart, I had double edged two knives.
I started to take up my flight,
Abruptly dragged down with all my might.

Astound to see the sudden shackles,
Tightly gripped in my ankles.
Oracle in sky like a storm of arrows from hulk's bow.
These shackles won't let me grow.

I howled and said...
"I am a rare race chiselled from pure yellow gold",
Do not dare to stop me from accomplishing my goal.
I can be as gentle as the soft wind caressing your face,
But do remember, I have a raging storm behind my grace.

FIROZ TATA (WOLFY)

I relaunched the flight; this time with fire,
Melting shackles, my knives unfurl the power of strong desire.
Finally, I saw my releasing long plight,
One day I'll surely be in peoples' light.

༶༶༶

21
His Lady

A lady with million hidden scars on her soul,
A lady quietly walking on a burning coal.
A lady scattering melting miraculous smiles and joy,
A lady with a dusk within, making him her lover-boy.
A lady born for zillion silent sacrifice,
A lady living her life in low light, paying else's price.

A daughter of a reckless greedy,
Childhood like a local cheap brandy.
Mother, a fitness freak,
Future not so safe and little bleak.
A lovely lotus born in mud,
A lady filled with beautiful blemished-blood.

A hearty healer, wishing to fall in silent blissed terror,
A heavenly grace, reflecting her naked soul in mirror.
A lover to be cherished forever,
A giver but never a receiver.
A golden caged bird destined for velvety sky,
Bondage dreams; drowning, dead and dry.

A lady worth the darling, powering sunrise from West,
A lady worth celebrating, until last breath leaves his chest.
A lady with a hurricane heart, glint eyes and holy forehead,
He didn't know she would be her life-long headache.
Blessed to relish her wondrous womanhood.
A lady born to be tenderly-strong, cherishing motherhood.

༄༄༄

22
Notion of an Ideal Nation

My fellow natives never sleep in agony and hunger,
My fellow sisters never live in dread and terror.
Where none of the innocents are slaughtered,
Poor's voice could be always herd.
Humanity must be our religion and need,
No discrimination based on class, caste and creed.
When we lent a helping hand to each other,
Making nation progress even further.

Children would play like colourful butterflies,
Swinging from tree to tree, enjoying the childhood's paradise.
Their tender minds are trained to learn curiosity,
Every child must be raised above adversity.
Divided into diverse directions is our motherland,
Path towards a single goal is the index finger of my hand.
Every single soul may move free like in their home,
Let's make our nation a love-land under one big dome.
A lone aim of correct today for brighter tomorrow,
Let's cement the cracks of yesterday, to avoid future's sorrow.

♡♡♡

23
Fitness

For the love of your body:
Staying active and fit is not that easy,
Need to stay away being food-drowsy.
Controlling cravings; stop being foodie,
Dumping laziness from life's dictionary.

Consistency is an effective formula,
Adding some efforts extra, love eating sweet 'santra'.
No room for reasons, but only results,
You have to hurdle mindless orthodox adults.

Not for the humiliation you are going through,
But your body demands care from you.
Don't get depressed from body's soreness,
It's just a start, train regular battling fattiness.

Diet enriched with proteins, carbs and fats,
Balanced ratio fleeing bad-health-bats.
Looking younger and youthful,
Unseen blow to a criticizer fool.

CLUSTERING RHYMES

Fitness and clean diet will make you happy,
Bestowing physical and mental health plenty.
Worry and despair shoved at the bay,
Instilling healthy habits, awards an aspiring ray.

Willpower and zeal for fitness is an ideal key,
Let the world see your charm and glee.
It's time to accept fitness as a hobby,
God has bestowed us a precious body.

❦❦❦

24
Sweeper's Story

A sad story:
This is my story, a poor dreamer,
Living meek life as a sweeper.
A wrecked hut at the suburban town,
My daughter, my diamond crown.

A family of three,
Cleaning roads, my daily chore.
Working too hard for some money,
Have to keep an account for every penny.

Having ends meat is a tough task,
There is no one to help, whom to ask?
Their kids go to public school,
My life, as slow as a mule.

Bottled-up under the burden of debt,
A better future to daughter, is a big threat.
Failed to fulfil; promises slaughtered,
Life bothered, blistered and blundered.

CLUSTERING RHYMES

Battling poverty; a tough task for my family,
Lives hanging by a thin thread miserably.
Wife suffering from a disease,
What future holds, makes me freeze.

Spending days, within a burning hope,
May God give some more strength to cope.
Struggling with the vicious cycle of penury,
Cursing my memory.

❧❧❧

25
Beauty and the Wolfy

When wolfy fall for the beauty:
If the world doesn't reach its eternity someday,
He hopes she finds her wolfy one day.
As the wrecking waves crash over and over,
Deeper and deeper she slips into a dark abyss.

For if her end was destined in a distant love-fire,
She'll be compelled to admit, "Yes, lover, I was a liar".
The ruddy melted mass that she'd be,
Unfortunately, she may never be revived again.

For if her end was destined through traumatic torture,
The inside-out beauty of her soul will always endure.
He'll treasure the warmth she used to hold,
For the one, his heart heartlessly got so cold.

Still he believes the tide will turn,
Wolfy-burns will go, and warmth will someday return.
His love will caress her curvy curves, like a varnish,
Bloodless wounds will give up and vanish.

CLUSTERING RHYMES

Into his arid heart if she dives,
Still she'll feel his wolfy vibes,
Perhaps not as bright as the shining sun,
But surely will bring her solace and great fun.

Staring at the sunset ocean once again,
Scripting his pain without any brain,
The 'Heart', once he mistakenly discovered,
His final resting place, will be always cheered.

ppp

www.ingramcontent.com/pod-product-compliance
Lightning Source LLC
LaVergne TN
LVHW021739060526
838200LV00052B/3363